T0041127

JOHN HARBISON

PIANO SONATA No. 2

This work was commissioned by Associated Music Publishers, Inc.

*The first performance was given on April 13, 2003 by Robert Levin
at the Celebrity Series, Jordan Hall, Boston.*

AMP 8193
First Printing: February 2005

ISBN 0-634-08027-X

Associated Music Publishers, Inc.

DISTRIBUTED BY

HAL•LEONARD®
CORPORATION
7777 W. BLUEMOUND RD. P.O. BOX 13819 MILWAUKEE, WI 53213

Program Note

My Piano Sonata No. 2 was completed at Civitella Ranieri, near Perugia, in May 2001. It was long in the works.

In 1994 I made a handwritten contract with Robert Levin, promising delivery of a sonata in 1995, at which point he would pay me one dollar. Much intervened, and the actual time of composition, around the first performances of my opera *The Great Gatsby*, was a turbulent period. New work for hire being scarce, I was able to work on various volunteer enterprises— a song cycle (*North and South*), a set of solo viola pieces, and most intently, this sonata. It was a source of joy and confidence when Susan Feder, Vice President of G. Schirmer, proposed that my publisher become the commissioner of the Sonata. The piece then became a talisman of two essential, long-lasting friendships; with its first performer and its commissioner(s).

In January 2001 I sent off a copy of the sonata with an odd feeling that something about the piece was missing. But such a feeling is not so unusual, and I went off to Civitella Ranieri intending to work on my Fourth String Quartet. During very late nights I began to hear what the Sonata was missing—no less than the heart, the mysterious center of the piece. The final variation movement does not "resolve" the sonata, but it opens it up by taking it inward. (My last day at Civitella Ranieri I remarked to a friend there how wonderful the all-hours privacy of the old granary was, my perfect dream of working unheard. "Are you kidding," she said, humming a fragment from the Variations, "for days every time we went by we heard that bit!").

I think of the Sonata as a not-always open letter to its first performer. For some years I have been interested in integrating my choral vocabulary—close points of imitation, canon, word-painting—into an instrumental setting emphasizing a long line with very few sectional divisions. I thought this fusion would interest Bob Levin, who is always acutely aware of every structural nuance from the most fleeting sonority to the most far-flung allusion. Since Levin is also a phenomenal improviser I wanted even the fanciest details to sound quasi-improvised, so that his cliff-hanging, risk-friendly performance style could flourish.

This piece includes immediate, rhetorical, explicit music with more reticent, conflicted music, and its character derives from the tension between them. In entrusting it to a dear friend and musician of incomparable gifts I had a sense of its being complete even before it was heard.

John Harbison

for Robert Levin

PIANO SONATA No. 2
I. Intrada

John Harbison

Tempo giusto, maestoso

♩ = 80–96

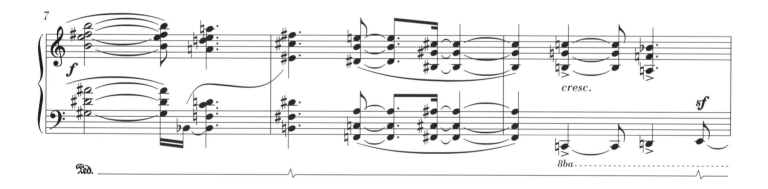

Con bravura

Copyright © 2003 by Associated Music Publishers, Inc. (BMI) New York, NY
International Copyright Secured. All Rights Reserved.
Warning: Unauthorized reproduction of this publication is
prohibited by Federal law and subject to criminal prosecution.

Declamando

Con bravura

Cantabile

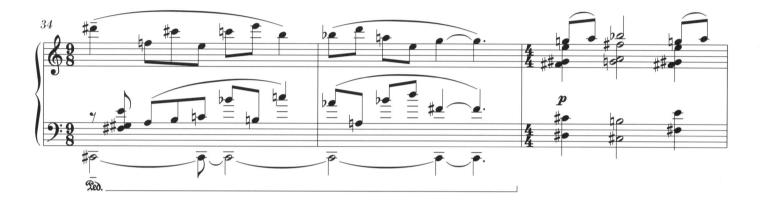

Chiaro, misterioso

Lucido

Campane lontane

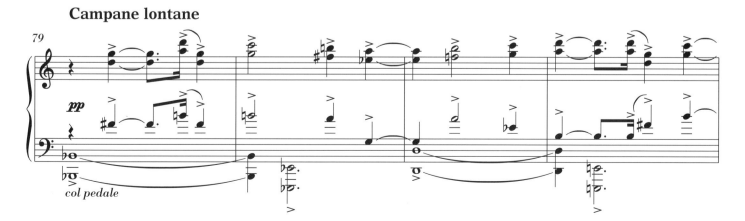

Declamando

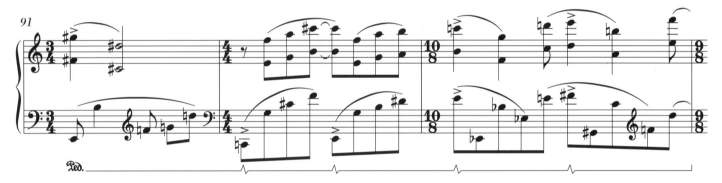

Con bravura

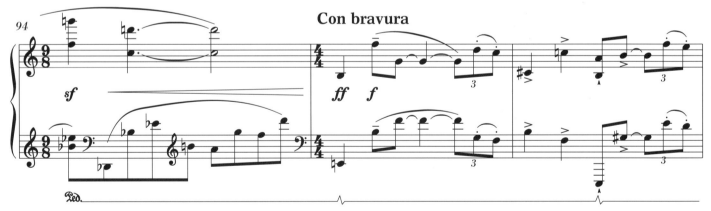

Limpido

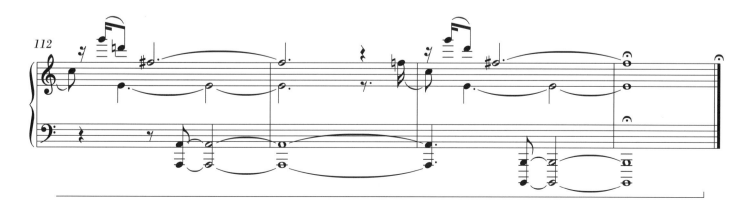

II. Aria

Luminoso, lucido

$\quad$ = 76

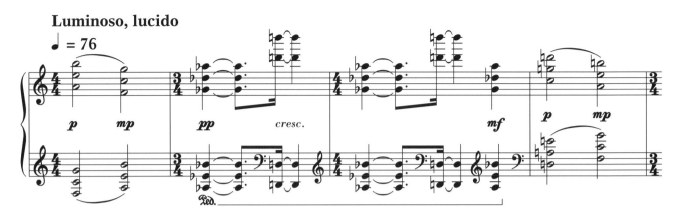

Rettorico

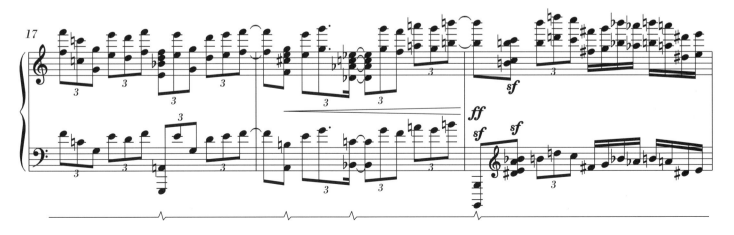

Trasparente

legato
accomp.

Con anima

Trasparente

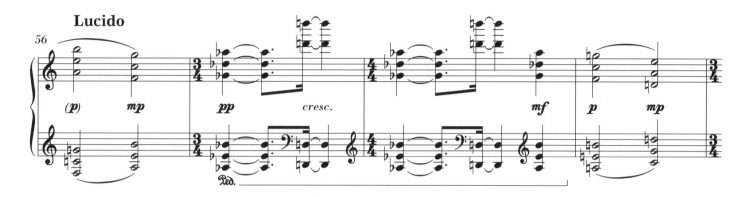

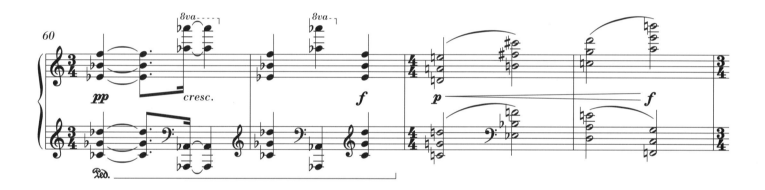

Con anima

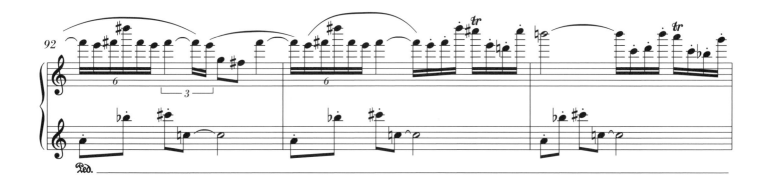

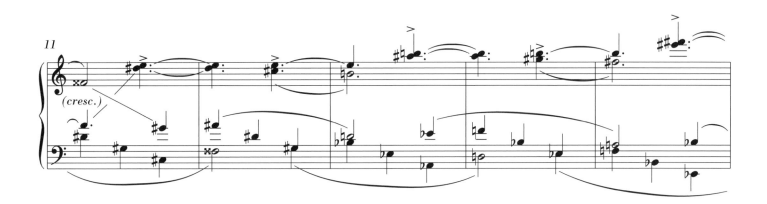

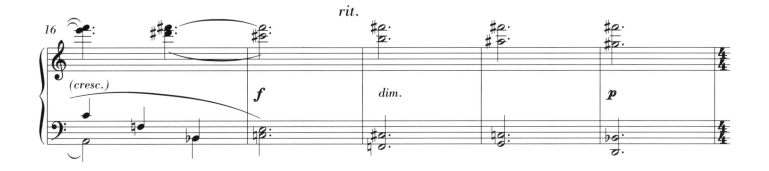

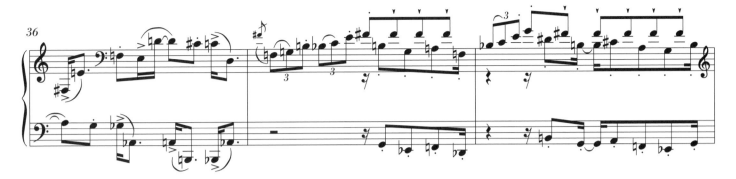

Feroce

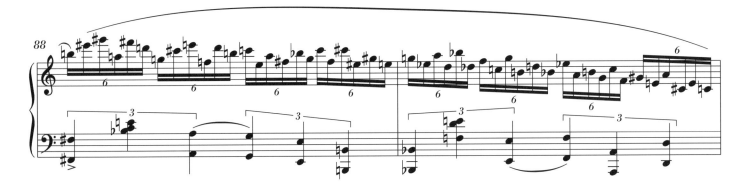

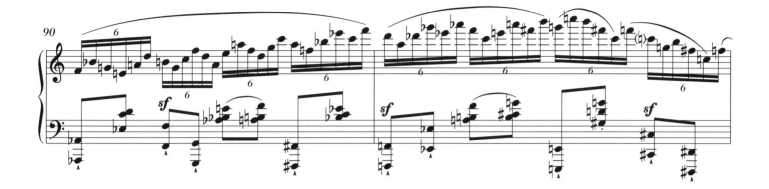

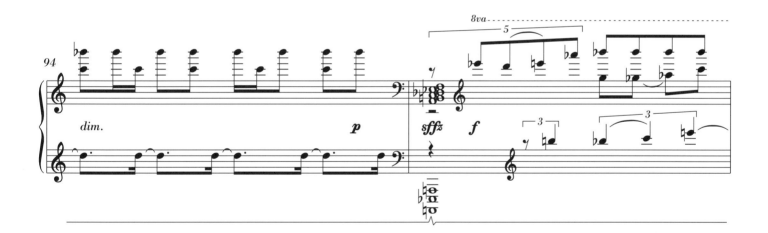

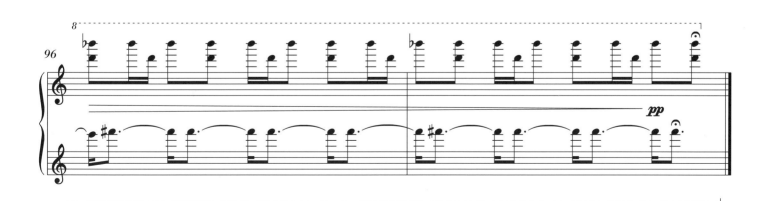

Var. 1

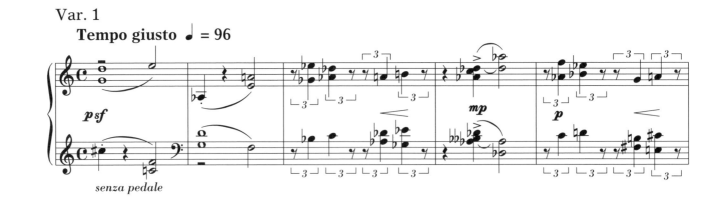

Var. 2

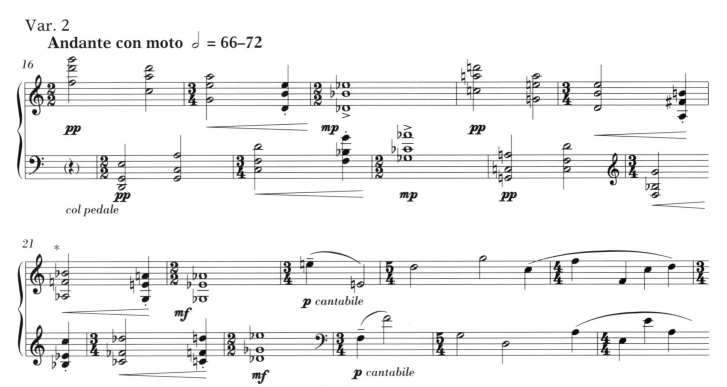

*Here and at measure 33, the hand distribution may be reassigned.

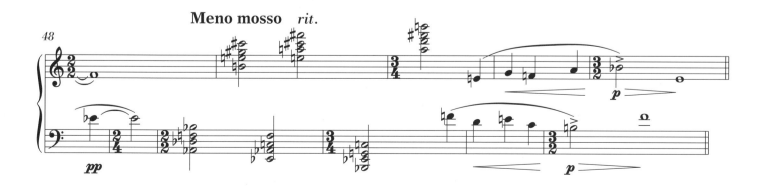

23

Var. 3

Andante affetuoso

♩ = 84–88

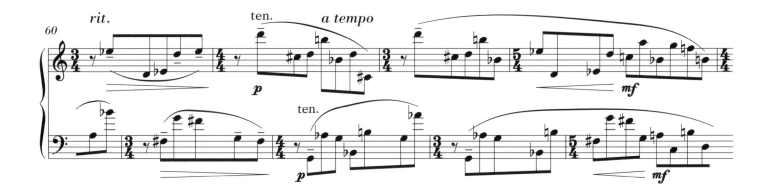

Var. 4

Larghetto sonoro

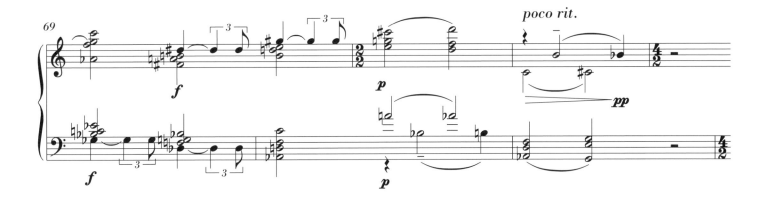

Var. 5

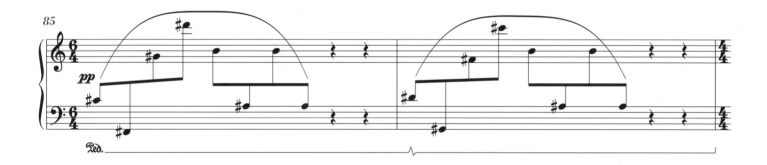

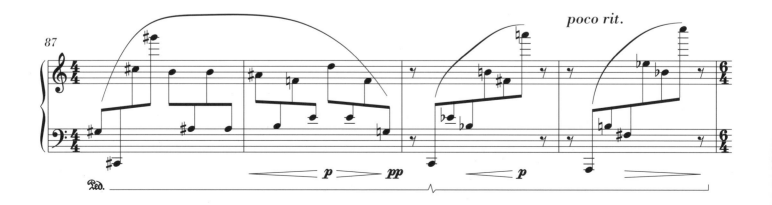

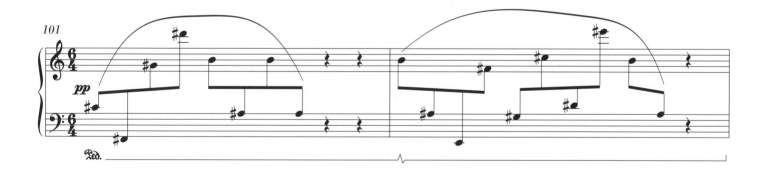

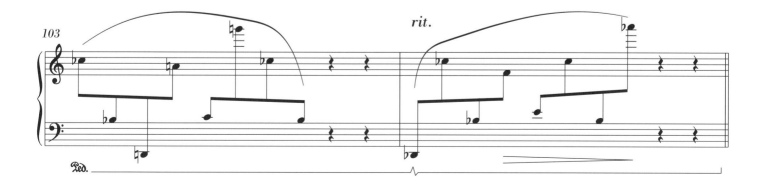

Var. 6

Allegretto misterioso ♩ = 96

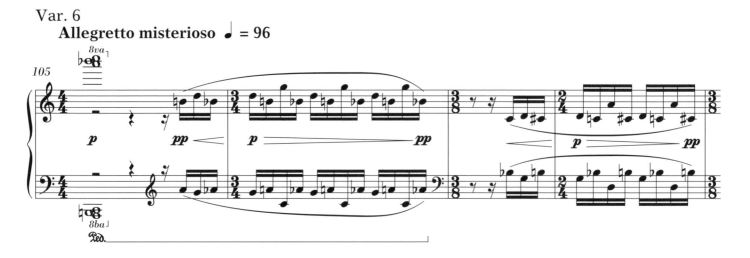

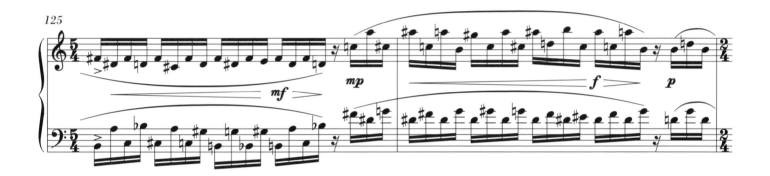

Var. 7

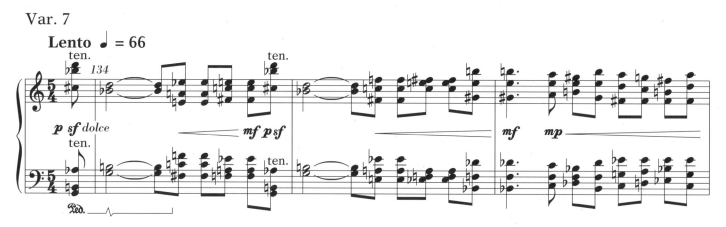